MICROWAVE
DOUGH
CRAFT

MICROWAVE DOUGH CRAFT

MORE THAN 50 ORIGINAL SALT DOUGH PROJECTS

ALISON JENKINS

APPLE

To Fiona, Gerry and Rob
A.J.

A QUINTET BOOK

Published by The Apple Press
6 Blundell Street
London N7 9BH

ISBN 1-85076-654-1

Reprinted 1996

This book was designed and produced by
Quintet Publishing Limited
6 Blundell Street
London N7 9BH

Creative Director: Richard Dewing
Designer: Ian Hunt
Project Editor: Alison Bravington
Editor: Alison Leach
Photographer: Paul Forrester
Illustrator: Wendy Thompson

Typeset in Great Britain by
Central Southern Typsetters, Eastbourne
Manufactured in Malaysia by
C.H. Colourscan Sdn. Bhd.
Printed in Singapore by
Star Standard Industries (Pte) Ltd

CONTENTS

Introduction 7

Equipment 8

Making and Baking Salt Dough 11

Techniques 14

PROJECTS

TEMPLATES AND CUTTERS 27

MOLDING 51

MODELING 77

DECORATIVE PIECES 97

Templates 116

Index 128

INTRODUCTION

The use of salt dough as a modelling medium has enjoyed an enormous increase in popularity over the past few years. Although its use is widely recognized as a folk art form throughout Europe and the USA, modelling with dough has far older origins. It is believed that the Ancient Egyptians, Greeks and Romans shared the tradition of offering baked bread dough models as tributes to their Gods. In a sense that tradition is still followed – many people are familiar with the bread wheatsheaves frequently displayed at Easter. Salt dough in the form we know today evolved in Europe during the nineteenth century as a progression from traditional bread doughs, the salt being added to protect models and decorations from being eaten by vermin.

Children and adults alike can enjoy a truly satisfying creative experience, using a material that is easily manipulated, highly versatile, inexpensive and non-toxic, to produce with a little imagination a limitless variety of durable models and decorations. The beauty of salt dough lies in its simplicity: the basic materials of flour, salt and water are readily available in most kitchens. Indeed all the projects featured in this book can be created at the kitchen table using only the most basic equipment.

Traditional dough craft methods involve the models being dried by baking in a conventional oven. While the results are undoubtedly successful, it may take up to 12 to 14 hours for a larger dough piece to be dry enough to paint. Using a microwave oven dramatically reduces the baking time; for example, a small piece can take mere minutes to dry while a larger one might take only a couple of hours or less. Although microwave dough craft could not be described as "instant" and still needs a certain amount of patience, the relative speed with which models can be created and finished is a definite advantage.

The ability to produce successful craft projects using a microwave oven requires a certain understanding of how this works. What then is the difference between a conventional oven and a microwave? Basically, in a conventional oven heat is generated outside the item to be cooked and is transferred through the container to the item; in a microwave oven the heat is generated from within the item itself. Microwaves are produced by a high frequency tube called a magnetron which is usually positioned at the top of the oven. The magnetron converts electrical energy into microwaves which are passed into the oven cavity and distributed evenly by a rotating fan. The microwaves are then reflected off the metal interior of the oven back to the item to be baked.

Salt dough and all foodstuffs contain moisture. When the moisture molecules are exposed to microwaves, they begin to oscillate at 2.5 thousand million times per second. This rapid vibration causes friction which in turn generates heat. This begins around the outside and slowly penetrates to the center. Smaller thinner items will therefore bake more quickly than larger thicker ones with a greater volume of dough. The understanding of this general principle will be invaluable when working with salt dough. All microwave ovens are different and a certain amount of experimentation will be required to produce successful results; the general rule is to err on the gentle side using lower power settings at first, thus giving much more room for error.

The projects in this book fall into three basic categories, each requiring different skill levels and techniques, beginning with simple templates and flat shapes, then progressing to more complicated moulding and modelling, providing instruction for the beginner and inspiration for the more experienced. Basic requirements, methods and techniques are described in the first chapter, followed by over 50 projects, each including a comprehensive equipment list and full step-by-step instructions.

EQUIPMENT

BASIC EQUIPMENT FOR TEMPLATES AND
——— FLAT SHAPES ———

FLOUR Use for kneading and for sprinkling over the pastry board and rolling pin to prevent the dough from sticking.

PASTRY BOARD A wooden one is best for rolling out dough.

ROLLING PIN Use for rolling out the dough to an even thickness.

PASTRY BRUSH Use to moisten the surface of the dough with water ready to attach other flat shapes or details.

SMALL KNIFE Use to cut out simple dough shapes and to cut around templates placed on the surface of the dough.

SCISSORS Use to cut out paper templates.

METAL CUTTERS The vast assortment of pastry, canapé and cake decorating cutters now available are invaluable for dough craft, especially for cutting out small or intricate shapes.

MODELLING TOOLS These plastic tools have pointed, blunt and rounded ends and blades are readily available from craft shops and are useful for cutting out fine shapes, smoothing out dough, making surface patterns and indentations.

WOODEN SKEWERS Use for making surface patterns and applying adhesive.

PAPER AND TRACING PAPER Use for tracing and cutting templates.

PENCIL Use for tracing templates and sketching.

BASIC EQUIPMENT FOR MOULDING
AND MODELLING

ASSORTED MOULDS Use microwave-safe dishes, plates and bowls as moulds; other objects such as egg shells and bottles can be used.

CARD AND CARD MOULDS Make your own moulds from thin card.

PLASTIC FOOD WRAP An essential item when moulding salt dough: a layer of plastic food wrap stretched over the mould will prevent the dough from sticking.

KNIFE Use for trimming edges of moulded shapes and for cutting out small shapes.

MODELLING TOOLS An assortment of plastic tools each differently shaped for cutting, modelling and surface decoration.

FORK The tines of a fork make even grooves when pressed into the surface of raw dough.

GARLIC PRESS Use to create texture.

MODELLING SYRINGE This has a number of different fittings enabling different shaped strands of dough to be extruded.

WOODEN SKEWERS AND COCKTAIL STICKS Use to create surface textures, apply adhesive and support small objects like beads for baking and painting.

SHELLS OR OTHER THREE-DIMENSIONAL OBJECTS Many objects can be used to emboss surface patterns – simply press the shape firmly onto the surface of the raw dough.

FABRIC Use for backings for small pictures.

WIRE Bend short lengths of wire into decorative shapes and use for embossing patterns into raw dough.

METAL CUTTERS Collect a variety of metal cutters to cut out flower petals, leaves, letters and other small shapes.

ADHESIVE TAPE Use masking tape to join card moulds together and double-sided tape for holding small shapes in position for painting.

FLORIST'S FOAM Press salt dough beads onto cocktail sticks and stick into florist's foam while the beads are being painted.

BASIC EQUIPMENT FOR PAINTING AND FINISHING

ACRYLIC CRAFT PAINTS AND SPRAY PAINT Non-water-based acrylic craft paints are ideal for decorating dough pieces as they provide good colour coverage and are quick drying.

OIL PAINT Use together with crackle varnish.

PAINTBRUSHES An assortment of different sized paintbrushes for applying paint and varnish.

TOOTHBRUSH Use to create a speckled paint effect.

SPONGES Use natural and synthetic sponges to produce a mottled paint effect.

POLYURETHANE VARNISH Available in gloss, matt and satin finishes; use to seal and protect finished dough pieces.

CRACKLE VARNISH A specialty varnish used to create an antique, crackled look.

QUICK-DRYING CRAFT ADHESIVE Use for fixing small light items such as beads to dough models.

EPOXY RESIN ADHESIVE Use this strong adhesive for repair work, for attaching small features to larger dough pieces and for fixing metal fittings.

STENCIL FILM Use this transparent plastic film for making stencils.

CRAFT KNIFE OR SCALPEL Use for cutting out stencils.

SANDPAPER Use fine grade sandpaper for smoothing rough edges and corners of baked dough pieces in preparation for decoration.

WIRE Bend short lengths of wire into decorative shapes for embossing; use finer wire for holding shapes together.

STRING AND RAFFIA Use to make decorative hanging loops for Christmas decorations and small pictures, and for attaching small dough pieces.

LEAVES The underside of a large leaf makes a delicate embossed pattern when pressed into the surface of raw dough.

NEEDLES AND SEWING THREAD Use for general sewing and attaching beads.

BEADS Use for embellishments and for Christmas decorations.

METAL FITTINGS Fittings such as magnets, jewellery findings, metal brackets, and brooch clasps are fixed to the painted models with epoxy resin adhesive.

MAKING AND BAKING SALT DOUGH

This chapter contains the basic salt dough recipe which has been used for every project in this book, and general guidelines to the preparation, baking and care of finished dough pieces. There are many recipes for salt dough, each requiring different proportions of flour to salt, and some including vegetable oil or wallpaper paste. However, this is the simplest recipe of all, and after much experimentation I have found it to be the most successful. For smaller amounts of dough, simply decrease your measure or for a larger amount increase the quantities, keeping the same proportions. Use plain flour, not self raising, as the raising agents will puff up during the baking process ruining your models, and use any finely granulated table salt. One cup of water is usually sufficient to bind the dry ingredients together. As you become more experienced, you will be able to judge exactly how much is required, perhaps a little more or a little less.

MAKING THE SALT DOUGH

INGREDIENTS
3 cups plain flour
1 cup fine table salt
1 cup cold water

EQUIPMENT
Mixing bowl
Measuring jug
Mixing spoon
Wooden pastry board
Plastic bag

Mix the flour and the salt together thoroughly with a spoon in a large bowl and then gradually add the cold water. Continue mixing until the contents of the bowl resemble a rough dough. Remove the dough from the bowl and knead thoroughly on a lightly floured pastry board for about 10 minutes until it is smooth and elastic and slightly warm to the touch.

Place the dough in a plastic bag to rest for about an hour. The dough can then be rolled out flat on a lightly floured wooden pastry board, moulded or modelled as the project requires.

TIPS
• Take care not to add too much water when making the dough as it will become too sticky and difficult to use.
• Salt dough will keep for about a week if placed in an airtight container or a sealed plastic bag inside the refrigerator. Always knead the dough again thoroughly on a floured pastry board after it has been in the refrigerator so it becomes soft and elastic again.
• Make sure that the rolling pin and pastry board are floured to prevent the dough from sticking. Always use plain flour, never self raising.

BAKING THE SALT DOUGH

When the dough piece has been completed, transfer it to the microwave oven for baking. If the piece has been made on a properly floured pastry board, it can be slid directly onto the turntable plate inside the oven, or, alternatively, carefully lifted using your hands, a spatula or a knife with a large flat blade. Place moulded and modelled pieces in the centre of the turntable plate; smaller pieces can be arranged evenly around the edge. Baking times vary greatly depending on the size, shape and thickness of the individual piece. Smaller thinner pieces generally cook more quickly than larger thicker ones. Surface area is also a contributory factor in

determining baking times. For example, you will find that a modelled piece with many small parts like leaves or flowers will dry out more quickly than one with a larger volume of dough but a smaller surface area such as a bowl or a large flat plaque.

As a rule, begin baking slowly on the lowest possible power setting and as you increase the power, decrease the baking time. Using a high power setting first will cause the model to swell and crack. Power output varies from model to model. Most microwave ovens are 650 or 850 watts. An 850-watt model was used for testing all the projects in this book. It is not usually necessary to use power settings higher than medium for baking salt dough. Baking times have been calculated on the following basis:

low:	80 watts
medium low:	150 watts
medium:	300 watts
medium high:	450 watts
high:	600 watts
full:	850 watts

Check the instruction manual of your microwave oven to assess which settings match the guidelines given here. A certain amount of experimentation may be necessary to discover how best to use your microwave oven.

Here is an example of the baking sequences suggested throughout the book: low for 20 minutes + 20 minutes, medium low for 10 minutes + 10 minutes, and medium for 5 minutes + 5 minutes. This means bake on low power for 20 minutes, leave to rest for a few minutes, and then bake again for an additional 20 minutes. Increase the power to medium low. Bake for 10 minutes, leave to rest for a few minutes, and then bake for an additional 10 minutes. Finally, increase the power to medium. Bake for 5 minutes, leave to rest for a few minutes, and then bake for an additional 5 minutes. By this time the piece should be dry enough, but if not, just leave to rest, then return to the microwave oven and repeat the last baking sequence.

Never leave the microwave oven unattended while baking is in progress because salt dough can scorch easily. Check the model at regular intervals, and allow a few minutes "rest" between baking periods. Remember that the dough will continue to dry out as it cools. If the dough begins to bubble or swell, stop the cooking process and let the piece rest. Then begin again.

When the dough is dry, it should be hard and crisp. Turn the model over and tap the underside with your index finger – it should sound hollow; if not, return the model to the microwave oven and repeat the last baking period until it is completely dry. It is easy to tell if a moulded shape is ready because the dough shrinks away slightly from the mould when dry. After the baking process is complete, remove the model and leave to cool completely before sanding and decorating. Do not attempt to remove a mould while the dough is still warm. Without the support of the mould the shape may warp as it cools.

TIPS
• If your model cracks slightly during the baking process, don't panic, just repair the damage by smoothing on a little fresh dough and then rebake to dry. Another method is to cover cracks or level out uneven surfaces using a light coloured wood filler – this will dry naturally without the use of the microwave oven. The repairs can be sanded down smoothly in the usual way. Other breakages can be repaired by using a strong epoxy resin adhesive.

SAFETY NOTES
• Always remember to use oven gloves when removing baked items from the microwave. Both the dough and the moulds can become very hot; also some items can give off steam which can burn your skin.
• Do not place metal containers or those with metal parts in the microwave oven as this may cause arcing which can damage the oven or cause a fire. Always make sure that any moulds used are microwave-safe. Tempered glass, ceramic, wood, microwave-safe plastics, rubber and cardboard are all considered suitable for use in the microwave oven. To test the suitability of a container, half fill with cold water and cook on high power for about 1 minute. If the water is hot and the container remains cool, then it is safe to use.

TECHNIQUES

The projects contained in this chapter serve as an introduction to dough craft, providing an excellent opportunity to develop skills and to practise decorative paint finishes.

———— TEMPLATES AND FLAT SHAPES ————

The beginner will find the use of simple templates and cutters an easy way to get started, as they help you to learn how to handle dough and to become familiar with using the microwave oven. Templates also form the basis of some of the more complicated projects featured later in the book. All the relevant templates needed for each project are included on pages 116–127. Trace off the outline and any decorative details onto a piece of plain paper, then cut out the design with a pair of sharp scissors.

1 Knead a ball of dough on a lightly floured pastry board. Using a floured rolling pin, roll out a thickness of approximately 5 mm (¼ inch) and place the paper template on top of the dough. Cut out and remove the inner areas first, using a small modelling knife, then cut around the template roughly with a larger knife. Carefully remove the waste dough from around the shape, place it in a plastic bag, and store in the refrigerator for future use.

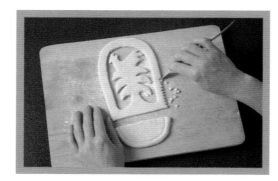

2 Use a small modelling tool to cut away small areas and to create finer details. Any surface details or decorations can be applied at this stage.

TIPS

• To create a rounded edge, press either your finger or a flat modelling tool along the edge of the dough.
• Flat shapes, sausage shapes and small details can be joined to the main piece by first moistening the surface with a little water to make it tacky, using your finger or a pastry brush for this. The two pieces can be pressed together. Smooth out the join with a modelling tool if necessary.
• The application of surface textures or indentations is not only decorative but aids the drying process by increasing the surface area, and also helps to keep pieces flat during baking. Make any holes for hanging loops and so on before the piece is baked. Pierce the dough with a wooden skewer or a cocktail stick.

MOULDING

With a little imagination an enormous variety of exciting decorative bowls, plates and containers can be made using everyday objects as moulds. Almost anything can be used providing it is microwave safe, from a ceramic plate to an eggshell. And if you cannot find a suitable mould, just make your own from thin card. All the projects featuring card moulds have trace-off templates (see pages 116–127). The salt dough form can be created in two ways: molding a flat dough piece or cutout shape, or building up the shape with sausage-shaped coils. Decorative or functional details such as rims, handles, bases, lids, relief and embossed patterns can be added to create imaginative and original pieces to keep yourself or for gifts.

MOULDING OVER A BOWL

1 First cover the outside of the bowl with a layer of transparent plastic food wrap – this will prevent the dough from sticking to the mould. Roll out a quantity of dough to about 5-mm (¼-inch) thickness on a lightly floured pastry board. Lift the dough carefully, supporting it underneath with your hand, and place over the inverted bowl. Press the dough gently down the sides of the bowl with your hands so it lies flat. Make sure that the dough is not too wet as it may stretch when lifted.

2 Trim the edge level with a small sharp knife. Press the blade of the knife gently against the edge of the dough after it has been trimmed to make a smooth edge. You can make a rounded edge by pressing your fingers along the cut edge.

MOULDING OVER AN EGG

Roll out a small quantity of dough on a lightly floured pastry board to about 5-mm (¼-inch) thickness. Cut out a large star-shape using a pastry cutter. Place the cut dough shape over an egg and smooth the points down each side.

1 Use a small bowl as a mold for both pieces. First mould, trim and bake a plain bowl shape. (See Moulding over a bowl, page 15.) Remove the dough shape from the mould and set aside – this will form the lower section of the bowl.

2 Using the same mould, repeat the process but this time cut away a circle of dough at the base of the mould (this will be the opening of the bowl). Roll out a sausage of dough about 1.5 cm (⅝ inch) in diameter and approximately long enough to fit around the cutout section (this will form the rim of the bowl). Use a modelling tool or small knife, cut the ends of the sausage diagonally so they will fit together neatly. Moisten the edge of the cutout section with water and press the rim in place.

3 Place the sausage around the cutout section, gently pressing into place. Make sure that the diagonally cut ends fit together neatly.

4 Using a modelling tool moistened with water, carefully smooth out the join between the rim and the bowl. Bake this upper section and then remove from the mould.

5 Place the two baked sections together and press small balls of raw dough over the join on the inside and the outside. Smooth out the raw dough with your fingers or a modelling tool moistened with water. Bake the shape again so all the dough is completely dry.

ADDING A BASE TO A BOWL

Press rolled-out dough or large cutout shapes over a mould. Roll out a sausage of about 1.5 cm (⅝ inch) in diameter, and long enough to form a circle at the base of the bowl. Use a knife or modelling tool to cut the ends diagonally so they will fit together neatly.

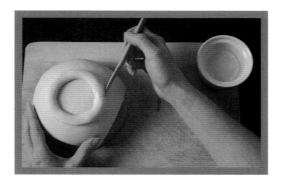

Moisten the surface of the dough around the base with a little water, then lightly press the sausage in place to form a circle. Smooth out the join between the base and the bowl with a modelling tool moistened with water. The same method can be used to add a base to vases or plates.

ADDING SURFACE TEXTURES

Add fine string-like relief patterns and textures to raw dough forms by using a modelling syringe. This is a clever tool used by model-makers to extrude dough, clay, or fondant frosting. It has a number of different sized and shaped fittings. Place a small amount of well-kneaded dough in the syringe, insert the plunger, and gently depress it to extrude the dough. You can "draw" a pattern directly onto the dough shape.

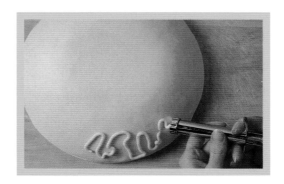

A wooden skewer is an invaluable modelling tool. Use the blunt end to make circular indentations into the surface of the dough. Not only does this create a decorative effect, but it also prevents flat shapes puffing up during baking.

Add a relief pattern by cutting circles of rolled-out dough into spirals using a small knife, then moisten the surface of the dough shape with water, and press the spirals into place. Smooth out the join with a modelling tool moistened with water, then add some decoration, using a wooden skewer. All flat dough shapes can be added to larger pieces in this way.

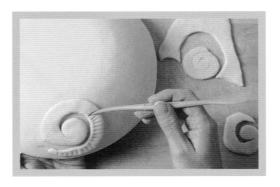

FREE MODELLING

Create elegant swirls by first rolling out a sausage-shape tapered at both ends, then pinching the shape between your thumb and forefinger to form a pointed ridge all the way along.

Curl up the shape from one end to form the swirl. Attach to the main dough shape or cutout by moistening the surface with a little water, then gently pressing the moulded piece into position.

STARFISH AND SHELLS

For a starfish, cut out a five-pointed star shape roughly, then pinch each point between your thumb and forefinger. Add surface textures with a cocktail stick or wooden skewer. For shells, roll out sausage-shapes tapered at one end and then roll up the shapes from the tapered end to form the shells. It is best to add the flat starfish to the model before baking, while the larger shell shapes are best baked first and then glued to the baked model using a strong epoxy resin adhesive.

LEAVES AND FLOWERS

For leaves, cut out leaf shapes using small pastry cutters or templates. Add surface texture by pressing the tines of a fork firmly into the dough or create veins by pressing the point of a modelling tool, skewer or cocktail stick into the surface of the raw rough. For rosebuds, cut out an oval or leaf shape using a cutter or template, and then flatten the dough between your fingers to make a larger thinner shape. Roll up the shape from one end to form a rosebud.

There are a great many small metal cutters available in flower, leaf and petal shapes, which are fun to use and very effective when combined with other surface textures. To make a large flower, roll out a quantity of dough quite thinly and cut out the required shapes. Build up the petal layers as shown. Squeeze a small quantity of dough through a garlic press to form the seeded centres of the sunflowers and daisies, scoop off the dough with a modelling knife, and lightly press the dough onto the flower shape. Using a modelling tool, wooden skewer or cocktail stick, press any surface details into the flowers and leaves when the dough is raw.

MAKING BEADS

Roll a small ball of dough into a sausage-shape about the diameter of the finished bead. Cut off equal sections of the sausage with a modelling knife and roll each one into a small ball. Thread the balls onto a wooden skewer and balance across the rim of a microwave-safe bowl. The beads can bake in the microwave oven in this way without distorting their rounded shape.

1

TEMPLATES
AND
CUTTERS

Bird-in-the-Bush

The charming little bird and tree motif in this candle sconce was inspired by Polish paper cuts popular in the nineteenth century. Use the sconce as a freestanding table ornament or hang it on the wall.

YOU WILL NEED

½ batch salt dough (see page 11)
Rolling pin
Flour
Pastry board
Tracing paper
Pencil
Scissors
Small knife
Modelling knife
Pointed modelling tool
Wooden skewer
Fine grade sandpaper
Acrylic spray paint
Newspaper
Acrylic paint in a darker colour
Mixing palette
Small piece of synthetic sponge
Paintbrush
Satin polyurethane varnish
Epoxy resin adhesive
Two small metal right-angle
     brackets
Empty casing of a nightlight
Small candle

SAFETY NOTE

• Never leave burning candles unattended. Always place candles on a heat-resistant surface and do not let candles burn down too low. Always use spray paints in a well-ventilated room.

● Roll out the dough to a thickness of 5 mm (¼ inch) on a lightly floured pastry board. Trace off the sconce and bottom templates on page 118. Cut out the template in paper and place on the rolled-out dough. Use a small knife to cut accurately around the base shape and roughly around the sconce. Using a smaller modelling knife, carefully cut around the bird and bush motif at the center of the sconce, removing the waste dough. Cut more accurately around the sconce shape and then using the modelling knife make tiny "V"-shaped cuts around the curved outside edge. Use a pointed modelling tool or a wooden skewer to make some decorative lines and features on the bird and the leaves of the bush.

● Roll a small ball of dough into a sausage about 1 cm (⅜ inch) in diameter. Cut it to fit around the outside edge of the base to act as a rim. Moisten the curved edge with water and then press the rolled sausage gently into place. Make rows of shallow indentations all over the surface of the base, using the blunt end of a wooden skewer. These indentations are not only decorative but will prevent the flat shape from rising and distorting during the baking process.

● Transfer the sconce and base to the microwave turntable plate and bake on low for 15 minutes + 15 minutes, medium low for 15 minutes, medium for 15 minutes, and medium high for 10 minutes. Remove from the microwave oven and leave to dry before decorating. Using sandpaper, smooth off any rough edges.

● Colour the sconce and base on both sides, using an acrylic spray paint. Place the pieces on a sheet of newspaper to protect your work surface. Leave the paint to dry before applying the darker colour. Spread a little of the darker paint onto a mixing palette and dip the sponge into the paint. Using a light dabbing motion, decorate the sconce and base with a subtle mottled pattern. Leave the paint to dry.

● Apply three coats of satin varnish to both sides of the sconce and base, leaving each coat to dry before applying the next.

● Attach the sconce back to the base, using strong epoxy resin adhesive. Hold the two pieces together in a right-angle position until the adhesive sets slightly. Use more of the epoxy resin adhesive to attach two small metal right-angle brackets to the join at the base of the sconce – the brackets will hold the join firm.

● Paint a nightlight casing to match the sconce and insert a small candle. Use strong epoxy resin adhesive to secure the casing in place on the base.

Tropical Fish Coat Hooks

A pair of brightly coloured tropical fish to adorn plain metal coat hooks.
Why not make a shoal of little fish, one for each member of the family.

YOU WILL NEED

¼ batch salt dough (see page 11)
Rolling pin
Flour
Pastry board
Tracing paper
Pencil
Scissors
Small knife
Fine grade sandpaper
Paintbrushes
Acrylic paint
Satin polyurethane varnish
Metal coat hook
Epoxy resin adhesive

● Roll out the dough to a thickness of 5 mm (¼ inch) on a lightly floured pastry board. Trace off the fish template on page 119. Cut out the template twice and lay both on top of the rolled-out dough. Using the small knife, cut roughly around the outside. Then remove the waste dough and, using the point of the knife, cut into the smaller areas around the fins and tail. Roll two small balls of dough for the eyes. Moisten the eye area with a little water and press each eye into position.

● Transfer the fish to the microwave turntable plate and bake on low for 20 minutes, medium low for 10 minutes, and medium for 5 minutes + 5 minutes. Remove from the microwave oven and leave to cool. Using sandpaper, smooth off any rough areas.

● Apply a base coat of acrylic paint to both sides of the fish shapes and leave to dry. Paint on the coloured features, using the photograph as a guide. When the paint has dried completely, apply three coats of satin varnish, leaving each coat to dry before applying the next.

● Screw the coat hook into position on the wall or on the back of a door. Attach the fish to the hook using epoxy resin adhesive.

Stone Brooch

An elegant brooch made from the simplest of dough shapes bound together with fine silvery wire. The subtle mottled paint finish gives an almost stone-like appearance.

YOU WILL NEED

⅛ batch salt dough (see page 11)

Rolling pin

Flour

Pastry board

Tracing paper

Pencil

Scissors

Small knife

Wooden skewer

Fine grade sandpaper

Paintbrush

Acrylic paints

Newspaper

Mixing palette

Toothbrush

Satin polyurethane varnish

Fine silver wire

Wire cutter

Brooch clasp

Epoxy resin glue

● Roll out the dough to a thickness of 5 mm (¼ inch) on a lightly floured pastry board. Trace off the brooch templates on page 118. Cut out the templates and lay them on top of the rolled-out dough. Using a small knife, cut around the templates. Pierce a large hole at the centre of each piece where indicated, using the blunt end of a wooden skewer.

● Transfer the pieces to the microwave turntable plate and bake on low for 10 minutes + 5 minutes, medium low for 5 minutes, and medium for 3 minutes. Remove the pieces from the microwave oven and leave to cool before painting. Using sandpaper, smooth off any rough edges.

● Apply two coats of acrylic paint to both sides of the brooch pieces (black and cream are effective colour combinations). Leave the paint to dry.

● Lay the pieces face upward on a sheet of newspaper. Place a small amount of paint on a palette, add water, and mix to a watery consistency. Dip the bristles of an old toothbrush into the paint and aim the brush at the dough pieces, drawing the blade of a knife toward you across the bristles. This will cause a fine spray of paint to be deposited on the surface (see page 25). Choose colours that contrast with the first coat.

● When the paint is dry, apply three coats of satin varnish, leaving each coat to dry before applying the next. When the varnish is dry, place the disk on top of the triangle and bind the two together by passing the wire through the centre hole and around the outside. Twist the ends of the wire on the reverse side to secure. Fix a brooch clasp to the reverse side, using epoxy resin glue.

Golden Baubles

Decorating the tree is always the best part of the Christmas festivities. These simple salt dough shapes have been sprayed with burnished gold paint and have tiny bead droppers attached with coloured threads.

YOU WILL NEED

¼ batch salt dough (see page 11) will make 10 or 12 decorations

Rolling pin

Flour

Pastry board

Heart, star and triangular shaped pastry cutters (large size for the main shape and smaller canapé size for the cutouts)

Bodkin

Fine grade sandpaper

Sheet of newspaper

Acrylic metallic finish spray paint

Paintbrush

Satin polyurethane varnish

Sewing needle

Coloured sewing thread

Small beads

● Roll out the dough to a thickness of 5 mm (¼ inch) on a lightly floured pastry board. Using the pastry cutters, stamp out heart, star and triangular shapes. Then using the smaller canapé cutters, stamp out a motif from the center of each one. Using a bodkin, pierce a hole for the hanging loop at the top of each decoration and also some holes to hang the beads from.

● Transfer half the decorations at a time to the microwave turntable plate and bake on low for 15 minutes + 15 minutes, medium low for 10 minutes + 10 minutes, and medium for 5 minutes + 5 minutes. Remove them from the microwave oven and leave to cool. Using sandpaper, smooth off any rough edges.

● Place the decorations on a large sheet of newspaper and spray the metallic paint on both sides, leaving the paint to dry before turning the shape over.

● Apply three coats of satin varnish to both sides, leaving each coat to dry before applying the next.

● Using coloured sewing thread, hang some small beads from the pierced holes. Pass four 20-cm (8-inch) lengths of thread through the hole at the top of each shape and tie the ends together to form a hanging loop.

> **SAFETY NOTE**
> ● Always use spray paints in a well-ventilated room.

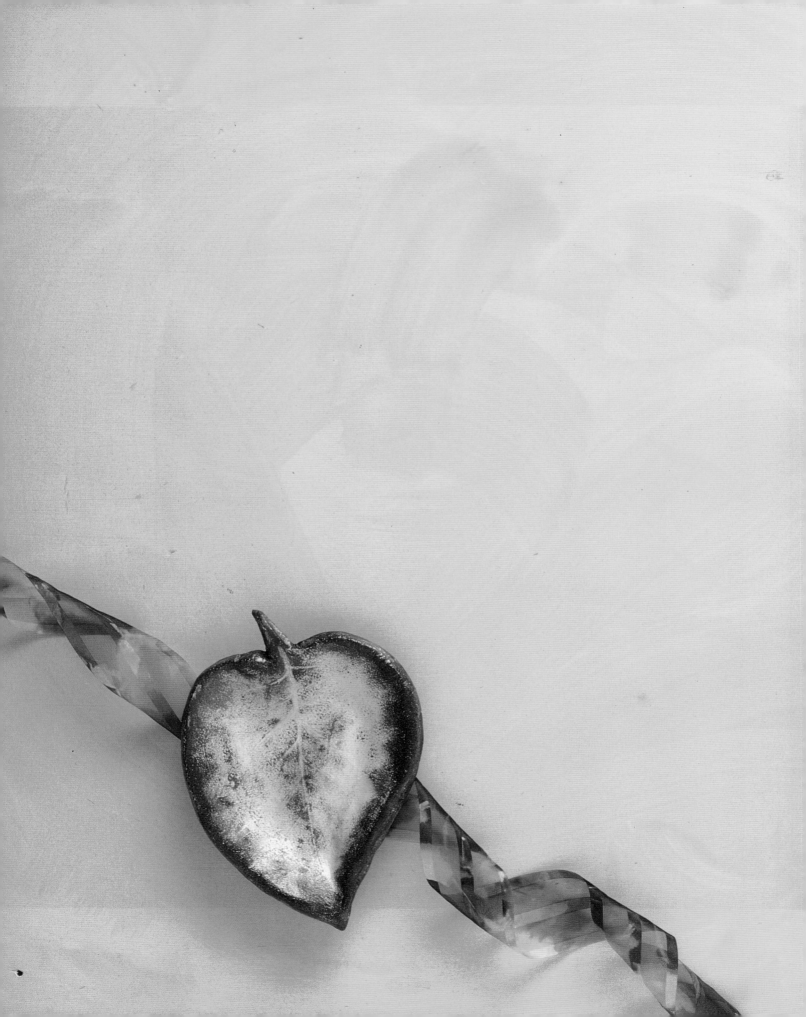

2
MOULDING

Coil Vase

*Salt dough vases make perfect containers for dried flower arrangements.
Fascinating, convoluted textures can be achieved by coiling rolls of raw salt
dough around a card mould. The uneven surface is further enhanced by using
contrast colours over the base coat.*

YOU WILL NEED

½ batch salt dough (see page 11)
Tracing paper
Pencil
Scissors
Thin card
Double-sided adhesive tape
Masking tape
Plastic food wrap
Rolling pin
Flour
Pastry board
Small knife
Modelling tools
Newspaper
Acrylic spray paint
Acrylic paint
Flat mixing palette
Small synthetic sponge
Paintbrush
Satin polyurethane varnish

● Trace off the card mould templates on page 121 and cut out the shapes in thin card. Bend the side piece to form a slightly tapered tube and join the side seam together with double-sided adhesive tape. Attach the round base to the mould, using tabs of masking tape (see Making and using card moulds, page 16). Cover the card mould with a layer of plastic food wrap to prevent the dough from sticking.

● Roll out a small ball of dough to a thickness of 5 mm (¼ inch) on a lightly floured pastry board. Use the original tracing of the base to cut out a small dough circle. Invert the card mould and place the dough circle over the base, pressing gently into position. Divide the remaining dough into balls and roll each one into a sausage shape about 1.5 cm (½ inch) in diameter. Coil the rolls around the mould beginning at the base, joining on new rolls of dough as you go. Continue coiling until you reach the edge of the mould (see Coiling around a mould, page 17).

● Using a moistened modelling tool, smooth out the joins between the coils (this will insure that they do not come apart during baking as well as making an interesting texture).

● Transfer the coiled mould to the microwave turntable plate and bake on low for 30 minutes + 30 minutes, medium low for 20 minutes + 20 minutes, and medium for 10 minutes + 5 minutes. Remove the mold from the microwave oven and leave to cool on the mould. Do not attempt to remove the mould while the dough is still warm, as this may result in warping and damage. Remove the card mould when the dough is completely cool.

● Place the dry dough vase on a large sheet of newspaper and use acrylic spray paint to colour the inside and the outside. Apply two coats if the coverage is not dense enough. Leave to dry. Spread a small amount of a contrasting colour paint onto a flat palette. Dip a small synthetic sponge into the paint and lightly wipe over the convoluted surface of the vase. The coloured paint will be deposited on the raised parts of the coiling, accentuating the irregular pattern and creating an interesting effect.

● After the decorative paintwork has dried completely, apply three coats of satin varnish, leaving each coat to dry before applying the next.

Greek Vase

This grand, urn-style vase with two elegantly curving handles is designed to hold a smaller glass vase or container. Fill the glass container with water so you are able to display fresh flowers of the season without damaging the salt dough.

YOU WILL NEED

1 batch salt dough (see page 11)
Rolling pin
Flour
Pastry board
Tracing paper
Pencil
Thin card
Scissors
Double-sided adhesive tape
Masking tape
Plastic food wrap
Small knife
Epoxy resin adhesive
Paintbrushes
Acrylic paints
Flat mixing palette
Small synthetic sponge
Satin polyurethane varnish

● Roll out the dough to a thickness of 5 mm (¼ inch) on a lightly floured pastry board. Trace off the tall vase template on page 121. Cut out the side and base in thin card. Bend the side to form a tapered tube and secure with double-sided adhesive tape. Attach the circular base with tabs of masking tape (see Making and using card moulds, page 16). Cover the card mould with a layer of plastic food wrap to prevent the dough from sticking.

● Place the original tracings on the rolled-out dough and cut around them with a small knife. Wrap the side shape around the card mould, pressing the straight edges together. Then place the circular base piece into position and press the edges together firmly. Trim the edge level with a small knife. Smooth out the joins and the cut edge with your fingers or a modelling tool moistened with water (see Making and using card moulds, page 16).

● Gather up some of the waste dough and roll into two 20-cm (8-inch) long sausage shapes about 2 cm (¾ inch) in diameter and tapering at both ends. Model each to form a "comma" shape (these will be baked separately and glued onto the vase afterwards to form the handles).

● Transfer the dough-covered mould and the handles to the microwave turntable plate. Make sure that the mould stands upside down, otherwise the dough will sag during the baking process. Bake on low for 30 minutes + 30 minutes, medium low for 20 minutes + 20 minutes, and medium for 10 minutes + 10 minutes + 5 minutes. Remove from the microwave oven and leave to cool. Do not remove the mould while the dough is still warm as this may cause damage and warping. Using sandpaper, smooth off any rough edges when the dough is completely cool.

● Fix the handles in position on either side of the vase, using a strong epoxy resin adhesive. Leave the adhesive to set hard.

● Apply two coats of acrylic paint in a pale colour to act as a base coat and a sealant. Take two contrasting coloured paints and spread a little of each onto a flat mixing palette. Use a small synthetic sponge to smear each colour lightly over the base coat. This creates a delicate mottled effect.

● When the decorative paintwork is completely dry, apply three coats of satin varnish, leaving each coat to dry before applying the next.

Ruby Red Conical Box

*A most unusually shaped box with a coiled lid and three curled legs, in which
to hide your treasures, richly decorated with deep reds and a hint of gold.*

YOU WILL NEED

½ batch salt dough (see page 11)

Rolling pin

Flour

Pastry board

Tracing paper

Pencil

Scissors

Thin card

Double-sided adhesive tape

Plastic food wrap

Small knife

Modelling tool

Fine grade sandpaper

Epoxy resin adhesive

Paintbrushes

Acrylic paint

Small sponge

Gold metallic acrylic paint

Satin polyurethane varnish

● Roll out the dough to a thickness of 5 mm (¼ inch) on a lightly floured pastry board. Trace off the conical template on page 121. Cut out the shape in thin card. Bend the card to form a cone and secure with double-sided adhesive tape. Cover the card mould with plastic food wrap to prevent the dough from sticking.

● Place the original tracing on the rolled-out dough and cut around it with a small knife. Wrap the dough around the conical mould and press the edges together. Smooth out the join with your fingers or a modelling tool moistened with water. Trim the upper edge level and smooth out the cut edge with your fingers or the blade of a modelling knife.

● Gather up the waste dough and roll into a sausage about 1.5 cm (½ inch) in diameter. Coil up the sausage to form a circle to fit the upper edge of the box (this will be the lid). Break off a small piece of dough and roll it into a small ball. Press it to the centre of the lid. Roll the remaining dough into three sausages about 15 cm (6 inches) long and coil each to form "S" shapes (these will act as legs for the box).

● Transfer the box, lid and legs to the microwave turntable plate and bake on low for 30 minutes + 30 minutes, medium low for 20 minutes + 20 minutes, and medium for 10 minutes + 10 minutes + 10 minutes. Remove from the microwave oven and leave to cool. Do not remove the card mould while the dough is warm as this may cause damage.

● Use strong epoxy resin glue to fix the three legs in place around the bottom of the conical box. Leave the glue to set.

● Apply two coats of acrylic paint to the box and lid and leave to dry. Sponge on some gold metallic paint lightly over the painted surface. When the decorative paintwork has dried, apply three coats of satin varnish, leaving each coat to dry before applying the next.

Fishy Dishes

These dishes make delightful wall decorations — each fish seems to have its own individual personality and facial expression. The use of simple templates and basic moulding methods again produce effective results, and the shallow concave shape offers a large area for creative decoration.

YOU WILL NEED

½ batch salt dough (see page 11)
    makes two dishes
Rolling pin
Flour
Pastry board
Tracing paper
Pencil
Scissors
Plain paper
Small knife
Two small saucers about 13 cm
    (5 inches) in diameter (moulds)
Plastic food wrap
Fine grade sandpaper
Paintbrushes
Acrylic paints
Satin polyurethane varnish

● Roll out the dough to a thickness of 5 mm (¼ inch) on a lightly floured pastry board. Trace off the fish template on page 122 and cut out as many shapes as you require in plain paper. Place the templates on the rolled-out dough and cut around the outside edge carefully using a small knife.

● Invert the saucers and place them on your work surface. Cover the convex side with a layer of plastic wrap to prevent the dough from sticking. Remove the turntable plate from the microwave oven and place one saucer in the centre. Carefully lift up one dough fish shape and place it over the inverted saucer mould. Smooth the dough with your fingers so it fits the convex shape. The template allows for a narrow rim around the outside of the saucer (this is indicated with a dotted line).

● Return the dough-covered mould on the turntable plate back to the microwave oven and bake on low for 20 minutes + 20 minutes, medium low for 20 minutes, and medium for 10 minutes + 5 minutes. Remove the dish from the microwave oven and leave to cool. Do not remove the saucer mould while the dough is warm as this may cause warping and damage.

● Prize the dish away from the mould, using a small knife, when it is completely cool. Using sandpaper, smooth off any rough edges.

● Apply two coats of white acrylic paint as a sealant and base coat to both sides of the dish. Leave to dry. Paint on details and features, using the photograph as a guide, or you could create your own designs.

● Apply three coats of satin varnish when the decorative paintwork is dry, leaving each coat to dry before applying the next.

Exotic Fruit Bowls

Bright orange and turquoise blue patterns lend these unusually shaped fruit bowls a slightly tropical flavour. Made by first cutting simple square and triangular shapes from rolled-out dough and then moulding over glass bowls of different sizes. Add a circular base to each to give character and stability.

YOU WILL NEED

1 batch salt dough (see page 11)
   makes one large bowl and two
   smaller ones
Rolling pin
Flour
Pastry board
Pastry brush
Plain paper
Pencil
Ruler
Scissors
Small sharp knife
Selection of round glass bowls
   in different sizes,
   one approximately
   2.5-litre (4-pint) capacity and
   two 600-ml (1-pint) capacity
Modelling tools
Fine grade sandpaper
Paintbrushes
Acrylic paints
Satin polyurethane varnish

● Divide the dough in half and then divide one half into two. Roll out each portion in turn to a thickness of 5 mm (¼ inch) on a lightly floured pastry board. On a plain sheet of paper draw out the square and triangular templates required for cutting the dough shapes: a 23-cm (9-inch) square for the large bowl and a 13-cm (5-inch) square and an equilateral triangle with 15-cm (6-inch) sides for the small bowls. Cut out the paper shapes and lay each in turn on to a rolled-out dough piece. Carefully cut around the outside of the paper template with a small sharp knife. Remove the excess dough.

● Invert the glass bowls and lay them flat on your work surface. Cover the outsides with a layer of plastic food wrap. Carefully lift each dough shape, supporting it underneath with your hand, and place it over the appropriate mould. Try to centre the dough pieces and gently smooth the corners flat down the side of the moulds.

● Then add a circular base to each of the bowls. Roll a small ball of dough into a sausage about 1.5 cm (⅝ inch) in diameter and long enough to form a circle at the base. Using a small knife, cut the ends of the sausage diagonally. Moisten the base area of each bowl and the cut ends of the sausage with a little water. Gently press the base into position, making sure that the ends are secure. Smooth out the joins, using a slightly moistened modelling tool (see Adding a base to a bowl, page 19).

● Transfer each dough-covered mould, one at a time, to the microwave turntable plate and bake the large bowl on low for 30 minutes + 30 minutes, medium low for 20 minutes + 20 minutes, and medium for 10 minutes + 5 minutes + 5 minutes; and the small square and triangular bowls on low for 20 minutes + 20 minutes, medium low for 10 minutes + 10 minutes, and medium for 10 minutes + 5 minutes. Remove them from the microwave oven and leave to cool, still supported by the mould. Do not remove the mould while the dough is still warm as this will cause warping. When completely dry carefully prize the dough bowls away from the moulds using a knife. Using sandpaper, smooth off any rough edges.

● Apply two coats of a light or neutral colour acrylic paint to act as a sealant and a base coat for the painted decoration. Using bright oranges and turquoise blues, paint bold swirls and spirals freehand on both the inside and outside surfaces.

● When the paintwork has dried completely, apply three coats of satin varnish inside and outside each bowl, leaving each coat to dry before applying the next.

Ribbon Dishes

The natural-looking free shape of these potpourri dishes is created simply by letting the moulded dough form its own shape around the glass or ceramic mold and leaving the edge untrimmed. Delicate paint effects using a natural sponge complement the softly curving form.

YOU WILL NEED

1 batch salt dough (see page 11)
    makes two bowls
Rolling pin
Flour
Pastry board
2.5-litre (4-pint) capacity glass
    bowl and a 1.2-litre (2-pint)
    capacity bowl to use as moulds
Plastic food wrap
Modelling knife
Small knife
Paintbrushes
Acrylic paints
Flat mixing palette
Small natural sponge
Satin polyurethane varnish
Two coloured ribbons

Use two-thirds of the dough for the larger bowl and the remaining one-third for the smaller one. Roll out the dough pieces to a thickness of 5 mm (¼ inch) on a lightly floured pastry board. Try to keep the pieces round or oval-shaped. Invert the glass bowls and place them on your work surface. Cover the convex side with a layer of plastic food wrap to prevent the dough from sticking to the mould.

Carefully lift up the rolled-out dough shapes and place on the relevant mould. Try to position the dough centrally. Gently press the edges of the dough so they lie smoothly around the sides of the moulds. Do not trim at this stage – just round off the wavy edge smoothly with your fingers or a moistened modelling tool. Cut eight small, irregularly-shaped holes about 2.5 cm (1 inch) from the rim of each dish, at least 4 cm (1½ inches) away from each other, to thread ribbon through when the dishes are finished.

Transfer each bowl separately to the microwave turntable plate and bake the large bowl on low for 30 minutes + 30 minutes, medium low for 20 minutes + 20 minutes, and medium for 10 minutes + 5 minutes + 5 minutes; and the small bowl on low for 20 minutes + 20 minutes, medium low for 10 minutes + 10 minutes, and medium for 10 minutes + 5 minutes. Remove them from the microwave oven and leave to cool on the moulds. Do not attempt to remove the dishes from the moulds while the dough is still warm as this may result in warping and damage. Carefully prize the dry dishes away from the moulds, using a small knife.

Apply two coats of acrylic paint in a light or neutral colour to both sides of the dough shapes as a sealant and base coat. When the paint is dry, spread a little paint in a contrasting colour onto a flat mixing palette. Dip the small natural sponge into the paint and press the sponge against the painted surface of the bowls. The irregular holes in the sponge will create a pleasing mottled effect. Decorate the inside and the outside of both bowls in this way.

When the decorative paintwork has dried completely, apply three coats of satin varnish, leaving each coat to dry before applying the next.

When the varnish is dry, thread ribbon through the holes around the rim of the bowl and finish by tying the ends together in a bow.

Embossed Wall Tiles

*With a little imagination you can find any number of three-dimensional
objects to be used successfully as embossing tools, from keys and wooden
clothes pegs to natural forms such as sea shells and leaves. A collection of
simple embossed salt dough tiles makes delightful wall decorations.*

YOU WILL NEED

½ batch salt dough (see page 11)
    makes four tiles

Rolling pin

Flour

Pastry board

Small knife

Assorted objects for embossing
    such as keys, wooden clothes
    pegs and shells

Wooden skewer

Paintbrushes

Acrylic paints

Small synthetic sponge

Satin polyurethane varnish

● Roll out the dough to a thickness of 5 mm (¼ inch) on a lightly floured
pastry board. Cut out four 12-cm (4¾-inch) squares, using a small knife. You
could make a paper template of a square. Create the embossed patterns by
pressing the keys, clothes pegs or shells firmly into the surface of the dough.
Take care not to press right through to the other side. Use a wooden skewer to
emboss a border groove about 5 mm (¼ inch) in from the cut edge around all
four sides and then use the end of the skewer to create the decorative dashes.
These indentations and embossed patterns are not only decorative but aid the
drying process and help to keep the dough shape flat during baking.

● Transfer the tiles to the microwave turntable plate and bake on low for
30 minutes + 30 minutes, medium low for 20 minutes + 20 minutes, and medium
for 10 minutes + 10 minutes + 5 minutes. Remove the tiles from the microwave
oven and leave to cool.

● Apply two coats of white acrylic paint to act as a sealant and base coat. Then
take two other colours and spread a little of each onto a flat mixing palette.

Using a synthetic sponge,
smear the paint lightly over
the base coat to accentuate the
embossed patterns. Make the
border a different colour.

● When the decorative paint
has dried completely, apply
two coats of satin varnish,
leaving each coat to dry before
applying the next.

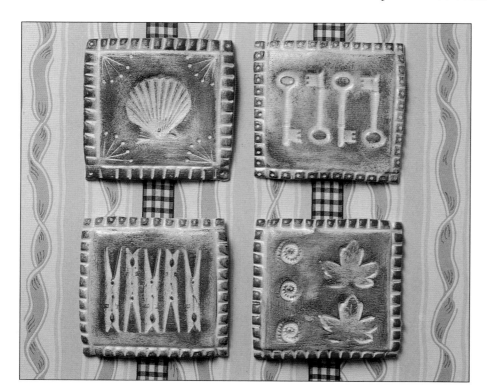

Embossed Trinket Box

*Keep your jewellery and trinkets safe inside this pretty little lidded box.
Moulded around a square glass bottle, the flat sides provide an excellent
surface for the embossed spiral decoration. Add a feminine touch by colouring
first in a rosy pink, then adding a blush of lilac.*

YOU WILL NEED

¼ batch salt dough (see page 11)

Rolling pin

Flour

Pastry board

Small square glass bottle (about
   6 cm (2½ inches) square) as
   a mould

Plain paper

Pencil

Scissors

Small knife

Plastic food wrap

Modelling tool

Wire coat hanger

Wire cutter

Fine grade sandpaper

Paintbrushes

Acrylic paints

Satin polyurethane varnish

● Roll out the dough to a thickness of 5 mm (¼ inch) on a lightly floured pastry board. Stand the glass bottle on a piece of plain paper. Trace around the base with a pencil and cut out the shape twice. Lay the paper templates on the rolled-out dough and cut around the edges, using a small sharp knife. Use one dough square as the base and the other as a lid.

● From the remaining dough cut a 6-cm (2½-inch) wide strip, long enough to fit around the circumference of the bottle. Cover the bottle with a layer of plastic food wrap to prevent the dough from sticking. Turn the bottle upside down and wrap the dough strip around the sides near the base. Press the short edges together to make a neat join. Place the square base onto the bottle mould and press the edges together. Smooth out the joins with a modelling tool moistened with water.

● Cut a 15-cm (6-inch) length of wire from a coat hanger, using a wire cutter. Bend the wire into a spiral shape, leaving a "tail" at the centre to use as a handle. Press the wire shape firmly onto the raw dough on each side of the box (see Embossed decoration, page 20).

● Take five small pieces of dough and roll each into a small ball. Use one as a knob for the lid and four as feet for the box. Moisten the centre of the lid and the four corners of the underside with water and press the dough balls gently into place. Transfer the dough lid and the bottle mould to the microwave turn-table plate. (You may need to support the bottle by standing it upside down in a mug or small dish to prevent it falling over as the plate revolves.) Bake on low for 20 minutes + 20 minutes, medium low for 10 minutes + 10 minutes, and medium for 5 minutes + 5 minutes. Remove from the microwave oven and leave to cool before removing from the mould.

● Slide the box from the bottle mould when it is completely cool. Using sandpaper smooth off any roughness.

● Apply two coats of acrylic paint to the box and lid as a base colour and sealant. Take a small amount of a contrasting colour paint on the end of your finger and rub over the painted surface to accentuate the embossed pattern. When the decorative paintwork is dry, apply three coats of polyurethane varnish, leaving each coat to dry before applying the next.

Burnished Bowls

*Bowls and containers moulded from salt dough are an excellent vehicle for all
types of surface decoration. Many pleasing and attractive results can be
achieved by using relief patterns made from dough applied in the raw state.
The spiral pattern shown here was made from a simple cutout shape while the
finer design was drawn on using a modelling syringe.*

YOU WILL NEED

1 batch salt dough (see page 11)
  makes two bowls
Rolling pin
Flour
Pastry board
Shallow ceramic bowls as moulds
  about 15–20 cm (8–10 inches)
  in diameter
Plastic food wrap
Small knife
Modelling knife
Modelling tool or cocktail stick
Modelling syringe
Fine grade sandpaper
Paintbrushes
Acrylic paints
Flat mixing palette
Small synthetic sponge
Gold metallic finish acrylic paint
Satin polyurethane varnish

● Divide the dough into equal portions. Roll out each to a thickness of 5 mm (¼ inch) on a lightly floured pastry board. Invert the moulds and cover the convex side with a layer of plastic food wrap to prevent the dough from sticking. Carefully lift up the pieces of rolled-out dough and place each on a mould, gently pressing the dough flat around the shape. Trim the edge level, using a small knife. Smooth the cut edge using your finger or a modelling tool moistened with water. Mould two bowls in this way.

● To make the relief decoration, gather up the waste dough and reroll to a thickness of 5 mm (¼ inch). Cut a small round of dough using a modelling knife and then cut each into a spiral shape. Moisten the surface of the moulded bowl with water and press the spiral shape into position. Smooth out the joins with a modelling tool moistened with water and then using a pointed modelling tool or a cocktail stick make decorative indentations around the spirals; this will help keep the decoration in place and also aid the drying process (see Adding surface textures, page 19). For the finer string-like decoration, place a small ball of dough inside a modelling syringe, insert the plunger, and gently squeeze to extrude a thin line of dough. "Draw" a pattern directly onto the moistened surface of the moulded bowl.

● Transfer the dough-covered moulds, one at a time, to the microwave turntable plate and bake on low for 30 minutes + 30 minutes, medium low for 20 minutes + 20 minutes, and medium for 10 minutes + 10 minutes + 5 minutes. Remove the moulds from the microwave oven and leave to dry. Do not remove the mould while the dough is still warm as this may cause damage and warping. When completely dry, prize the dough bowl from the mould. Using sandpaper, smooth off any rough edges when the dough is completely cool.

● Apply two coats of acrylic paint to each of the bowls as a sealant and base colour. Then spread two toning colours on a mixing palette and using a small synthetic sponge, smear the two colours randomly over the painted surface. When the paint has dried, apply gold metallic paint in the same way, to highlight the relief decoration and create an interesting mottled effect inside the bowls. Leave the decorative paintwork to dry thoroughly.

● Apply three coats of satin varnish, leaving each coat to dry before applying the next.

Two-Piece African Bowl and Vase

These earthy, African-inspired bowls are unusual in that the shape tapers inward toward the top. If a mould of this shape were used, it would be impossible to remove it without destroying the dough shape. Therefore these particular bowls have to be made in two pieces and joined to form the complete shape.

YOU WILL NEED

1 batch salt dough (see page 11)
    makes two
Rolling pin
Flour
Pastry board
Small ceramic bowls to use as
    moulds, about 13 cm (5 inches)
    in diameter
Straight-sided terracotta
    flower pot
Plastic food wrap
Small knife
Modelling knife
Fine grade sandpaper
Paintbrushes
Acrylic paints
Flat mixing palette
Small synthetic sponges
Scissors
Satin polyurethane varnish

• Divide the dough into quarters and roll out each portion to a thickness of 5 mm (¼ inch) on a lightly floured pastry board. Cover the convex side of the ceramic bowl with plastic food wrap to prevent the dough from sticking. Lift a piece of rolled dough and place it on the mould, pressing the dough with your fingers so it lies flat. Trim the edge level using a small knife.

• Transfer the dough-covered mould to the microwave turntable plate and bake on low for 20 minutes + 20 minutes, and medium low for 15 minutes + 15 minutes. When the dough is almost dry, remove from the microwave oven and leave to cool. Do not remove the mould while the dough is still warm as this may cause damage and warping. Prize the dough shape carefully from the mould with a small knife when it is completely cool and keep to one side. This will form the base of the bowl.

• Repeat the moulding process with another piece of dough but this time cut a circle around the base (this will form the upper part of the bowl). Roll a small ball of waste dough into a sausage about 1.5 cm (½ inch) in diameter and long enough to fit around the opening. This will form the rim. Trim the ends of the sausage at right angles to make a neat join. Moisten the edge of the opening with a little water and gently press the rim into position, pressing the trimmed ends together. Using a moistened modelling tool, smooth out the joins. Bake the upper part as before and remove from the mould.

• Place the two parts of the bowl together and press small balls of raw dough to cover the join, inside and outside. Using a modelling tool moistened with water, smooth out the join. Return the bowl to the microwave oven to dry the fresh dough join, baking on low for 30 minutes, medium low for 20 minutes, and medium for 20 minutes. When dry, remove from the oven and leave to cool. Using sandpaper, smooth off any roughness around the joined area.

• Apply two coats of acrylic paint in a terracotta colour as a sealant and base coat. Then paint the upper part and the rim black. Using a small sponge and cream-coloured acrylic paint, make a mottled pattern over the darker upper area. Cut another piece of sponge into a "V" or triangular shape. Dip it into the paint and use it to make the other bold patterns running around the side of the bowl.

• When the paintwork has dried, apply three coats of satin varnish inside and outside, leaving each coat to dry before applying the next.

VASE
• Repeat the process described for the bowl, but mould the bottom half over a straight-sided terracotta flower pot.

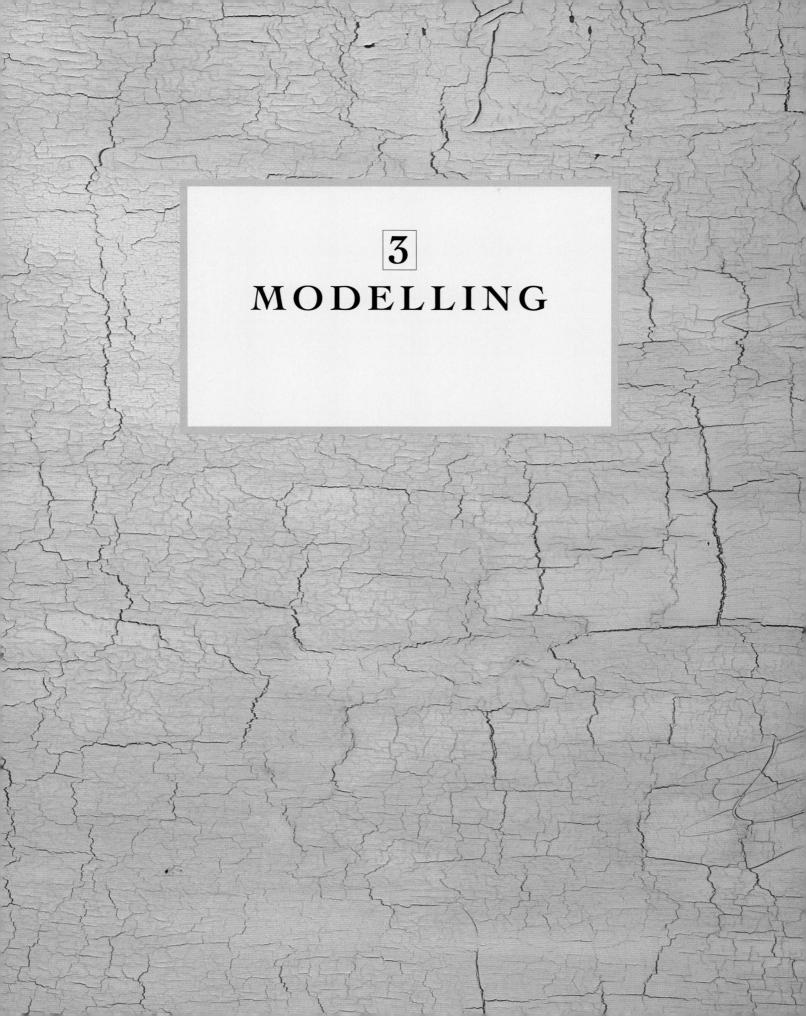

3
MODELLING

Daisy Pictures

Fresh as a daisy! These three-dimensional flower pictures make a pretty pair when hung together on a wall. The natural hessian backing gives a pleasing country look.

YOU WILL NEED

¼ batch salt dough (see page 11)
    makes two
Rolling pin
Flour
Pastry board
Large petal-shaped cutters
Small round canapé cutter
Cocktail stick
Garlic press
Paintbrushes
Acrylic paints
Satin polyurethane varnish
Short lengths of narrow
    wooden edging
Two 10-cm (4-inch) squares of
    plywood
Wood glue
Moulding pins
Hammer
Hessian fabric
Double-sided tape
Two blocks of wood about
    2 cm square x 1.5 cm deep
    (¾ inch x ½ inch)
    Epoxy resin adhesive

● Roll out the dough to a thickness of 3 mm (⅛ inch) on a lightly floured pastry board. Using the large petal cutters, stamp out about 24 petals for each flower and using the canapé cutter, one round centre. Remove the excess dough and place a row of petals around each centrepiece. Pinch the points of each petal and then use a cocktail stick to make a groove in the centre. Add a second row of petals in the same way as the first (see Leaves and flowers, page 23). Place a small ball of dough in a garlic press and scoop the resulting strands onto the centre to resemble seeds.

● Transfer the flowers to the microwave turntable plate and bake on low for 10 minutes, medium low for 5 minutes + 3 minutes, and medium for 2 minutes + 1 minute. Remove them from the microwave oven and leave to cool.

● Apply two coats of white acrylic paint to both sides of each flower to act as a sealant and base coat. When the paint is dry, apply three coats of varnish, leaving each coat to dry before applying the next.

● Make a square frame from the wooden edging to fit the plywood backing. Glue together and then use moulding pins to keep in place. Paint the frame brown. Cut a square of hessian to fit inside the frame and attach, using double-sided adhesive tape. Attach the small blocks of wood to the centre of each frame using epoxy resin glue. Secure the flower on top which creates a three-dimensional effect.

Aztec Mask

A stunning wall decoration created by moulding and layering simple template shapes combined with surface texturing techniques. The earthy yellows, reds and greens blend so well together to produce a strikingly authentic effect.

YOU WILL NEED

1 batch salt dough (see page 11)
Rolling pin
Flour
Pastry board
Tracing paper
Pencil
Plain paper
Scissors
Small knife
13-cm (5-inch) diameter saucer to
    use as a mould
Plastic food wrap
Modelling tools
Wooden skewer
Fine grade sandpaper
Paintbrushes
Acrylic paints
Small synthetic sponge (optional)
Satin polyurethane varnish

● Roll out the dough to a thickness of 5 mm (¼ inch) on a lightly floured pastry board. Trace off the basic template on page 123, and then trace off the other template details following the solid lines (the dotted lines represent surface details). Cut out the templates in plain paper and place on the rolled-out dough. Cut around each shape, using a small knife, removing the eye and mouth sections. Remove the excess dough.

● Cover the convex side of the saucer with plastic food wrap and lay it on the pastry board. Carefully lift the main mask template and place it over the mould. The saucer should fit under the face part of the mask and the head-dress should lie flat on the board. Moisten the entire surface of the dough with water and carefully lay the other cutout shapes in position.

● Use modelling tools or a wooden skewer to make the surface decorations, referring to the dotted lines on the template and to the photograph as a guide. Use a moistened modelling tool to smooth out the joins. The raised details on the forehead and earrings are made from small balls of dough squashed to make a flatter shape and then pierced with the blunt end of a skewer. For the nose, model a small ball of dough into a pyramid shape and press it carefully into position, smoothing out the joins with a moistened modelling tool. Form the nostrils, using a pointed modelling tool.

● Transfer the mask to the microwave turntable plate and bake on low for 20 minutes + 20 minutes, medium low for 20 minutes, and medium for 10 minutes + 10 minutes. Remove it from the microwave oven and leave to cool. Do not attempt to remove the mould while the dough is still warm as this may cause warping and damage. Gently prize the dough mask away from the mould and, using sandpaper, smooth off any rough edges.

● Apply two coats of beige acrylic paint to both sides of the mask to act as a sealant and base coat. Apply the other decorative colours, using the photograph as a guide. Use a dry brush or a sponge to achieve the subtle effects.

● When the decorative paintwork is dry, apply three coats of varnish, leaving each coat to dry before applying the next.

Rose Wreath

This decorative piece with textured leaves and rose buds was inspired by the modelled bread dough wreaths made in Crete. The tradition of bread dough modelling is one that dates back to ancient times – this particular example translates well into salt dough form and is not as complicated to make as it looks.

YOU WILL NEED

1 batch salt dough (see page 11)

Rolling pin

Flour

Pastry board

Plain paper

Pencil

Scissors

Small knife

Small leaf-shaped pastry cutters

Fork

Cocktail stick or fine
    modelling tool

Paintbrush

Satin polyurethane varnish

● Roll out the dough to a thickness of 5 mm (¼ inch) on a lightly floured pastry board. Cut out a 23-cm (9-inch) diameter circle in plain paper to use as a template for the base. Cut another circle about 13 cm (5 inches) from the centre. Place the paper ring on the rolled-out dough and cut around it.

● Gather up the excess dough and reroll to the same thickness. Using a pastry cutter, stamp out plenty of rounded leaf shapes and press the tines of a fork firmly into the surface to make deep grooves. Press the leaves around the outside and inside circumference of the dough ring. Cut out a large number of pointed leaf shapes. Using a cocktail stick or a fine modelling tool, trace on the veins. Place these leaves on the dough ring just inside the first rows. For the rose buds, cut out an oval leaf shape and press flat. Roll up the flat shape to form the flower. Place the flowers in groups of three or four around the ring. Fill in any gaps with tiny rose buds or leaves (see Leaves and flowers, page 23).

● Transfer the wreath to the microwave turntable plate and bake on low for 30 minutes + 30 minutes, medium low for 15 minutes + 15 minutes + 15 minutes, and medium for 10 minutes + 5 minutes + 5 minutes. Remove the wreath from the microwave oven and leave to cool.

● Apply three coats of satin varnish to both sides of the wreath, leaving each coat to dry before applying the next. This particular model has been left unpainted to show the natural colour of the dough. It is important, however, to make sure that all the convoluted surfaces of the shape are completely sealed with varnish.

Deep Sea Dish

*The subtlety of the blue and gold shades combined with the delicate shapes of
starfish and shells used to decorate the dish create a wonderful effect that
reflects the beauty of the undersea world.*

YOU WILL NEED

1 batch salt dough (see page 11)

Rolling pin

Flour

Pastry board

Ceramic dinner plate to use
    as a mould

Plastic food wrap

Small knife

Modelling tools

Cocktail stick

Epoxy resin adhesive

Paintbrushes

Acrylic paints

Gold metallic acrylic paint

Flat mixing palette

Sponge

Polyurethane varnish

● Roll out the dough to a thickness of 5 mm (¼ inch) on a lightly floured pastry board. Cover the concave side of the plate with plastic food wrap to prevent the dough from sticking. Carefully lift the rolled-out dough and place it on the plate, pressing it into place with your fingers so the dough follows the concave shape. Trim around the edge of the plate, using a small knife, and smooth out the cut edge with your fingers or a moistened modelling tool.

● For the starfish, gather up the excess dough and reroll a little thinner than before. Cut out about 15 small five-pointed star shapes, using a small knife. Pinch each point between your thumb and forefinger. Add the textured detail with the point of a cocktail stick or a fine modelling tool (see Adding surface textures, page 19). Moisten the rim of the dish with a little water and press the starfish shapes onto the surface. For the seaweed, cut narrow pointed strips and press onto the surface. For the shells, gather up the remaining dough and roll into sausage shapes, tapered at one end. Roll up from the narrow end to form the shell. For the limpets, model a small ball of dough into shallow cone shape and, using a cocktail stick, add the decorative lines.

● Transfer the plate mould to the microwave turntable plate. Place the shells and limpets on the oven plate separately and bake on low for 20 minutes + 20 minutes, medium low for 10 minutes + 10 minutes, and medium for 5 minutes + 5 minutes + 5 minutes. Remove from the microwave oven and leave to cool. Do not remove the plate mould while the dough is warm as this may cause damage and warping. When completely dry, prize the bottom plate away from the mould with a small knife. Using sandpaper, smooth off any rough edges.

● Attach the dough shells in place, using strong epoxy resin adhesive. When the adhesive has set, apply two coats of light blue acrylic paint to both sides of the dish to act as a sealant and base coat. Use a sponge to apply darker colours to the outside and underside of the dish in a mottled subtle pattern and richer mid blues to the centre and to accentuate the curves of the shells. Paint the starfish gold and apply a delicate gold blush with a sponge to the rest of the dish.

● When the decorative paintwork is dry, apply three coats of satin varnish, leaving each coat to dry before applying the next.

Sun and Moon Bookends

Plain wooden bookends are given a celestial touch with silvery crescent moons set on a background of the sun's golden flames.

YOU WILL NEED

1 batch salt dough (see page 11)
Rolling pin
Flour
Pastry board
Tracing paper
Pencil
Plain paper
Scissors
Small knife
Modelling tool
Wooden skewer
Fine grade sandpaper
Sheet of newspaper
Paintbrush
Gold and silver metallic
    acrylic spray paints
Satin polyurethane varnish
Approximate 60-cm (2-foot)
    length of 6-cm (2½-inch) wide
    softwood
Small hacksaw
Hammer
Small nails
Epoxy resin adhesive

● Roll out the dough to a thickness of 5 mm (¼ inch) on a lightly floured pastry board. Trace off the sun and moon templates on page 124. Cut out two of each shape in plain paper and place the templates on the rolled-out dough. Cut around the templates, using a small knife.

● For the suns, pinch each pointed flame shape between your thumb and forefinger to make rounded edges and then bend each a little to resemble flickering flames. For the moons, round off the outside edge, using your fingers or a moistened modelling tool. Using the photograph and design lines suggested on the template, build up the features, using modelling tools and small pieces of dough on the moistened surface of the moon. The eyebrows and lips are thin tapered sausages of dough. Form the eyes by pressing a ball of dough into position and then make a hole in the centre with the blunt end of a wooden skewer. The eyelids are a semicircle of dough pressed into place with a modelling tool.

● Transfer the suns and the moons in pairs to the microwave turntable plate and bake on low for 30 minutes + 30 minutes, medium low for 20 minutes, and medium for 5 minutes + 5 minutes + 5 minutes. Remove the shapes from the microwave oven and leave to cool. Using sandpaper, smooth off any rough edges.

● Place the dry dough shapes on a sheet of newspaper and apply two coats of acrylic spray paint to each side. Colour the moons silver and the suns gold.

● When the paint is dry, apply three coats of satin varnish to both sides of each shape, leaving each coat to dry before applying the next.

● To make the bookends, cut four pieces of wood about 13 cm (5 inches) long and then using epoxy resin glue, stick together to form two right angles. Cut two small triangles from the remaining wood and glue in position to support the angles. When the glue has set, nail the wooden pieces together securely and spray with gold acrylic paint.

● Use epoxy resin adhesive to attach first the sun to the support triangle of each bookend and then the moons on top.

Tulip Key Holder

Tulips and tiny forget-me-nots give this pretty wall decoration a fresh springtime feel. Not only attractive but functional too, the terracotta coloured base has a row of tiny hooks to keep your house keys safe.

YOU WILL NEED

½ batch salt dough (see page 11)
Rolling pin
Flour
Pastry board
Tracing paper
Pencil
Plain paper
Scissors
Small knife
Small flower- and leaf-shaped
    cutters
Garlic press
Wooden skewer
Paintbrushes
Acrylic paint
Sponge
Satin polyurethane varnish
Hand drill with small bit
Small brass screw-in hooks

● Roll out the dough to a thickness of 5 mm (¼ inch) on a lightly floured pastry board. Trace off the templates for the base and leaves on page 124 and cut out in plain paper. Lay on the rolled-out dough and cut around the base template, using a small knife. Then cut out about 12 large leaf shapes and about 8 smaller ones. Remove the excess dough and reroll a little thinner than before. Using small cutters, stamp out more leaf shapes and some forget-me-nots.

● Place the large leaves in a row growing up from the top of the base. Pinch the pointed end of each and curve each one slightly for a more realistic effect. Do the same with the smaller leaves, placing them over the bases of the first. Put a small ball of dough into a garlic press and arrange the resulting strands of dough around the base of the leaves to resemble moss. Add some more small leaves, making the veins with a modelling tool, and then add some tiny forget-me-nots, piercing the centre of each with the blunt end of a wooden skewer. Roll small balls of dough into egg shapes for the tulip blooms. Place these on the leafy background and roll very thin sausage shapes to act as stems for each bloom.

● Transfer the model to the microwave turntable plate and bake on low for 15 minutes + 15 minutes, medium low for 10 minutes + 5 minutes, and medium for 3 minutes + 3 minutes + 3 minutes. Remove it from the microwave oven and leave to cool. Using sandpaper, smooth off any rough edges.

● Apply two coats of acrylic paint to both sides of the model as a sealant and base coat. Colour the leaves and flowers green and the base terracotta. Follow the photograph as a guide and use your imagination for the other decorative details. Sponge on a light sheen of cream-coloured paint to highlight the modelled shapes.

● When the decorative paintwork is dry, apply three coats of varnish, leaving each coat to dry before applying the next.

● Finally, drill four small holes at the base of the model and screw in the brass hooks.

4

DECORATIVE PIECES

Fringed Lamp Shade

*A plain lamp shade can be given an unusual decorative touch by suspending
flat triangular dough shapes from the bottom.*

YOU WILL NEED

¼ batch salt dough (see page 11)

Rolling pin

Flour

Pastry board

Tracing paper

Pencil

Plain paper

Scissors

Small knife

Cocktail stick

Fine grade sandpaper

Paintbrushes

Acrylic paints

Satin polyurethane varnish

Bodkin

Fine black cord or coloured string

Lamp and lamp shade

● Roll out the dough to a thickness of 5 mm (¼ inch) on a lightly floured pastry board. Trace off the template shape given on page 126 and cut out as many shapes as you need in plain paper. Place the templates on the rolled-out dough and cut around each one, using a small knife. Remove the excess dough. Round off the edges of each shape with your fingers and pierce a small hole at the top, using a cocktail stick.

● Transfer the shapes to the microwave turntable plate and bake on low for 10 minutes + 10 minutes and medium low for 5 minutes + 5 minutes. Remove the shapes from the microwave oven and leave to cool. Using sandpaper, smooth off any rough edges.

● Apply two coats of light coloured acrylic paint to both sides of each shape to act as a sealant and base coat. Then paint on a contrasting colour and any details, using the photograph as a guide or choosing your own patterns.

● When the decorative paintwork is dry, apply three coats of varnish, leaving each coat to dry before applying the next.

● Using a bodkin, pierce a row of small holes through the lamp shade around the bottom. Tie on each shape with a small piece of fine cord or coloured string.

Mexican Candlesticks

Lizards and firebirds are typical design motifs of Ancient Mexico. The stylized, uncomplicated outlines lend themselves very well to template work. Paint matt black and then add a spattering of gold to create a burnished appearance.

YOU WILL NEED

¼ batch salt dough (see page 11)
Rolling pin
Flour
Pastry board
Tracing paper
Pencil
Plain paper
Scissors
Small knife
Modelling tools
Fine grade sandpaper
Paintbrushes
Acrylic paint
Pair of candlesticks
Sheet of newspaper
Gold metallic acrylic spray paint
Satin polyurethane varnish
Strong epoxy resin adhesive

● Roll out the dough to a thickness of 5 mm (¼ inch) on a lightly floured pastry board. Trace off the lizard and firebird templates on page 126. Trace the relief decorations (the areas tinted cream) separately. Cut out each shape in plain paper and place on the rolled-out dough. Cut around the shapes, using a small knife, and remove the excess dough. Moisten the surface of the main shapes with water and gently press the relief decorations into position. Using a modelling tool, smooth out the joins.

● Transfer the shapes to the microwave turntable plate and bake on low for 15 minutes and medium low for 5 minutes. Remove them from the microwave oven and leave to cool. Using sandpaper, smooth off any rough edges.

● Apply two coats of black acrylic paint to both sides of the shapes to act as a sealant and base coat. Paint the candlesticks black too (acrylic paints are very versatile and will adhere to most surfaces including metals and plastics). Then place the candlesticks and dough pieces on a sheet of newspaper and lightly spray with gold metallic paint.

● When the decorative paintwork is dry, apply three coats of varnish, leaving each coat to dry before applying the next. Attach the decorations to the candlestick stems using epoxy resin adhesive.

Tulip Basket

Decorate a plain wicker basket with little tulip motifs painted with checks and spots for a country look.

YOU WILL NEED

⅛ batch salt dough (see page 11)
Rolling pin
Flour
Pastry board
Tracing paper
Plain paper
Pencil
Scissors
Small knife
Fine grade sandpaper
Acrylic paint
Brushes
Mixing palette
Acrylic spray paint
Newspaper
Satin polyurethane varnish
Epoxy resin adhesive

● Roll out the dough to a thickness of 5 mm (¼ inch) on a lightly floured pastry board.

● Trace off the tulip template given on page 127 and cut as many as you need from plain paper. Lay the templates onto the rolled out dough and cut around the outside using a sharp knife.

● Transfer to the microwave turntable plate and bake low for 10 minutes, and medium low for 5 minutes. When the dough is dry, remove from the microwave oven and allow to cool. Using sandpaper, smooth off any rough edges.

● Apply two coats of acrylic paint to both sides of the tulip shapes to act as a sealant and base coat. Then with a contrasting colour paint, add checked and spotted details. When the decorative paintwork is dry, apply three coats of varnish, leaving each coat to dry before applying the next.

● Place the wicker basket on a large sheet of newspaper and apply one or two coats of acrylic spray paint. When the paint is dry, fix on the dough motifs using epoxy resin adhesive.

Fishy Dishes

page 63

Dotted line indicates

position of saucer

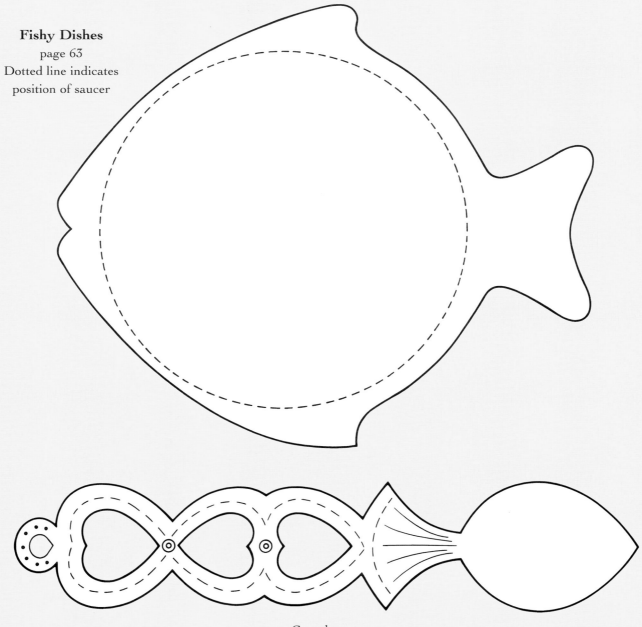

Complete spoon

Welsh Love Spoons

page 80

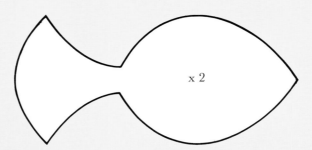

Spoon bowl

Aztec Mask
page 83
Dotted lines
represent
surface detail

**Underwater World
Wall Decoration**
page 89

Sea horse
x 4

Seaweed

Place to fold

Place to fold

Fringed Lamp Shade
page 99

Carrot

Spring onion

Chilli

Vegetable Pots
page 100

Lizard

Mexican Candlesticks
page 102
Areas tinted
cream represent
relief decoration

Shell

Seashore Boxes
page 106

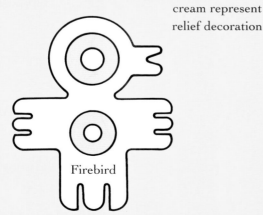

Firebird

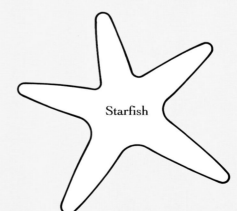

Starfish

Jeweled Boxes
page 110

Tulip Basket
page 115